One Thing Sixty-Six-Day Workbook

One Thing Sixty-Six-Day Workbook

PUBLISHER: BLACK DOG PUBLISHING, ATLANTA, GEORGIA

Author: Steven Monahan

ISBN-13: 978-1540856142

ISBN-10: 1540856143

Printed in the USA

# Contents

Introduction: When the Sun Rises

Part One: Finding Your One Thing

Chapter 1: Living Your One Thing

Chapter 2: The Nature of You

Chapter 3: Writing Your Story

Chapter 4: Myers–Briggs

Chapter 5: Sixteen Personality Types

Chapter 6: Learning Styles

Chapter 7: A Clear Path

Part Two: Achieving Your One Thing

Chapter 8: How Do I Start?

Chapter 9: Why Do You Want Your One Thing?

Chapter 10: Dig Deep

Chapter 11: Hierarchy of Needs

Chapter 12: Focus

Chapter 13: Introverts and Extroverts

Chapter 14: How You Spend Your Days

Chapter 15: Good Habits


Part Three: Maintaining Your One Thing

Chapter 16: Two Wolves

Chapter 17: The Shift

Chapter 18: How to Kill Your Dream

Chapter 19: Live in the Present

Chapter 20: Hang Out with Uplifting People

Chapter 21: Start with Gratitude

Chapter 22: Never Stop


Closing Thoughts

About the Author

# Introduction
## When the Sun Rises

"When the sun rises, I go to work.

When the sun goes down, I take rest.

I dig the well from which I drink.

I farm the soil which yields my food.

I share creation. Kings can do no more."

—Chinese proverb

We all want one thing. We all want to live a meaningful life. How we do that is the makings of religion, teachers, gurus, science, and self-help books. We spend more money on the attempt to find happiness and a meaningful life than we spend on anything else. We look within, and we look outside. We buy things, and when they don't bring the desired result, we buy something else. We get external things to fill an internal want. We find spouses; we get jobs. We have kids. We get pets, houses, cars, things, and more things to fill what is lacking in our inner souls and minds. But whatever we acquire, the feeling of satisfaction eventually wears off. So we keep searching. There is something missing. There is always still one thing missing. What is it? It's the one thing you were meant to be. The one thing you were designed to do. This workbook will help you start to see how to look for it and where to look for it, and hopefully, it will set you on a path to it.

We all want to wake up in the morning eager to face the day and start doing the thing—the one thing—that makes us happy, energized, and fulfilled. We know we can find our one thing. We know we can live a meaningful life. Why? Because we see people doing it.

I am going to go out on a limb here. I'm going to guess that because you bought *The ONE Thing* book by Gary W. Keller and Jay Papasan and now this book, your desire is to live a meaningful life.

Three years ago, I bought and read *The ONE Thing*. I found it to be a life-altering book. Others have obviously felt the same—it has made more than four hundred appearances on national bestseller lists. It won twelve book awards, has been translated into thirty languages, and was chosen as one of the Top 5 Business Books of 2013 and one of Top 100 Business Books of All Time by Goodreads.

The idea of doing one thing is elegant and straightforward. The book says that to live the meaningful life you desire, do one thing. Throughout the book, it lays out why the one thing is the way to achieve this desire. It talks about the Pareto 80/20 rule, the power of focus, and the need to decide what it is you want, then lay out the dominos and knock one over each day. It talks about the ability to use habits over willpower—to do your one most important thing today, and then tomorrow, do your one most critical thing that day, and so on and so on.

After I read *The ONE Thing*, I was engaged. I was energized. I felt its message was so clear and so simple that I would incorporate it into my work as a career-change coach.

I led a discussion on the concept of simplicity and doing one thing at the Mastermind business group I lead. I had my clients read it. Just a few months into teaching its message, I found something interesting, however. I saw a pattern emerge.

People loved the book and its "one thing" concept. But—and this was the big *but*—they could not figure out how to apply the "one thing" concept to their personal situation. They would ask me questions like these: How do I choose my one thing? What questions must I ask? How do I uncover my skills and talents? How do I choose just one thing, the career I was made for?

I understood exactly how they felt. A few years earlier, I was in the same situation. At age fifty-three, and after a twenty-five-year career in the corporate world, I found myself at the top of the ladder, right where I had planned to be and had worked tirelessly to achieve throughout my entire career. Was I happy? Yes . . . and no. I was happy I made it, but I was unhappy because when I achieved my goal, it felt hollow and meaningless. I knew that I had a very difficult choice to make: to play it safe and ride the merry-go-round for another ten years or jump off while the merry-go-round was still spinning.

It took me a year to dig deep and come to my answer. It was an emotional decision, a reasoned decision, and a big financial decision. I weighed all the angles . . . and then I jumped. I left the safety net. I had to jump, take a risk, and find my one thing again. I felt that if I were to keep doing something that was not fulfilling, my soul would shrivel and die. So I left the structured and safe corporate world and became an entrepreneur. I moved from playing it safe to taking a risk. From having a structure to work within to having no structure at all, to having to create it as I moved along.

What did I do? I opened an executive search and career-change business. I had no professional background in human resources. In the corporate world, I was a senior vice president, the general manager over many disciplines, not just one. I hired hundreds of people throughout my career. I managed and led the same numbers. I was a coach and mentor, but I was never a human resources specialist.

Now I was a specialist and doing one thing, not many things. And the amazing thing is this: it was just what I was searching for. It was a tighter focus. It was doing the one thing I felt and saw clearly that I was designed for. Working one-on-one with people to help them find new careers and build new lives woke my soul again. Had I not jumped off the merry-go-round, had I not put it all on the line, I would have never found my one thing. When I left my career in finance, my friends and associates were stunned. Many people say they want more than what they have, but few are ready to leave the safety net and jump into the abyss to find it.

When I left the company, I engaged a career coach. We talked in depth, and I went through a battery of tests. We spent time talking about my skills, my traits, and my natural talents. We also spent time on what I did not excel at or find of interest. Finding the perfect one thing takes some work.

Part of the process involved a battery of psychological tests, such as the Myers–Briggs, the 16 Personalities, and others. Through them, I started to see who I was . . . and who I was not. The Myers–Briggs testing showed that I was an ENTJ type, which represents the main attributes of extroverted, intuitive, thinking, and judging. It was clear I could only find the creative freedom I needed by being an entrepreneur, not working in a monolithic corporate structure. It showed me what I had inwardly sensed the year before I left my lifelong career. I had to be constantly challenged and fully engaged in work and life to live a life of meaning. Coasting or resting on my laurels for the next few years of my career was not in my psychological makeup.

Let's be clear on this. To have a truly purposeful, rewarding, full, and happy life, to use our God-given talents and our learned skills to their fullest potential, we must live one undivided life. A full life. We cannot achieve our genius by living two lives and doing or being two things.

Finding your one thing is finding yourself. And expressing that self is done through your vocation—what you do. You want your vocation to be your vacation.

This workbook is focused on helping you uncover your one thing to live your right livelihood and therefore a meaningful and purposeful life. This book will help you start to see a clearer picture of who you are. It will bring to your attention your born gifts and your created skills. It will help you to discover elements of your personality, your talents, and your temperament, and with that, it will help you find the career—the vocation—that fits you perfectly.

When you live your natural talents, your passions, and your purpose, you will live your right livelihood. Finding your one thing is the same as finding your right livelihood. Living your right livelihood is utilizing your natural talents, the things you're made of—it is like always being in the zone. When I found my right one thing, I finally felt comfortable with who I was. I felt like I had finally met the real me and we were reunited old friends. When you find your one thing— and you will—and fully utilize your skills and natural tendencies, you will say, "This is exactly what I was meant to do, who I was born to be."

# Part One: Finding Your One Thing

## Self-exploration: personality tests

# Chapter 1
## Living Your One Thing

When you are living your one thing, your life is enhanced. It is mentally, spiritually, and physically fulfilling. The right one thing nourishes your talents, skills, and sensibilities. It simply suits you and clearly reflects who you are. It allows you to use your natural abilities. Life flows and doesn't stumble. Synchronous things happen. How do you know if you have chosen the career that nourishes your one thing and allows your life to flourish? This is how you will know if you are doing the right one thing:

• You will feel excited and optimistic each day and for the future.

• You will enjoy the people in your life, your work, and whomever you meet on your path.

• You will feel that your work and knowledge and skills are appreciated and respected.

• You will feel proud of your vocation and your work.

• Your work will energize you, not drain you.

• You will look forward to each day to apply your skills, talents, and natural abilities for not only your own good but the good of others as well.

Let me make this clear. There is no golden, one-of-a-kind one thing that fits all people. There is, however, one thing that is just for you. Like the proverbial snowflake, we are all different, all totally unique. My one thing will not be your one thing, and vice versa.

There is an infinite number of one things. To find the one perfect for you, all you need to know is who you are. You are your own clue to finding your one thing. Find out what your talents, skills, and preferences are, and you will find your one thing, perfectly suited to you. Some one things bring stability. Some bring risk. Some require extroverted desires; some are better suited to introverted sensibilities.

As you will see in this workbook, there are sixteen main personality types and many combinations of attributes that form who we are. Plus, we all have different drivers and markers. Some want money; some want to contribute to society. I love searching. I love learning. Others want stability and enjoy sticking to what they know. I feed off a good debate; others only want agreement. The differences among us are vast, but that is what makes life fun.

When you know yourself, you will find yourself. Finding your own one thing is not as hard as many imagine. It only takes knowing who you are, what you are good at, and what you are not. It does take effort, however. This is your one thing, and only you can find it and accept it. I can help, and I can give you the clues, but you must do the inner work so that the answer comes from you, not from me.

One big clue is to ask yourself this: Do I feel natural doing it this way? Try this old but faithful experiment. On a clean piece of paper, write your name with your favored hand. For most, that is the right hand. Then turn the paper over and write your name with your opposite your hand—let's say your left hand. How comfortable were you when you used your preferred hand? Did it feel easy, natural, and effortless, or did you have to think and struggle?

Now think about how it felt when you used your opposite or unnatural hand. Was it difficult, slow, draining, or tiring? Did it require effort and thought?

Now transfer that to your present vocation or job or one thing. How do you feel when you are doing your one thing? Are you energized? Does it feel effortless and natural?

Or do you feel that it's a struggle, unnatural, draining, or tiring?

Forget what others want you to be or tell you to be. Be who you are. You can never be fulfilled being someone else. Shakespeare said it well: to thine own self be true.

Flee from people who belittle your ambitions. Small people always do that, but the really great make you feel that you, too, can become great."—Mark Twain

# Chapter 2
## The Nature of You

*A tree is known by its fruit; a man by his deeds. A good deed is never lost; he who sows courtesy reaps friendship, and he who plants kindness gathers love.*

—*Saint Basil*

Everything alive has a nature to it—what, by nature, it naturally is. A tree was meant to be a tree. It must therefore be a tree. An oak tree does not try to be a rock or a stream.

Everything is created to naturally be its own one thing. A bird has one purpose—its one thing: to be a bird and fly. To fly naturally, with no effort or strain, through the air. To swoop and soar and simply be a bird that thrives in the sky, its natural environment.

A fish also has its own one thing: to be a fish and swim in the water. It breathes only in the water. Its natural home is water, not the sky. Out of water, a fish will die. In water and out of the sky, a bird will struggle and soon die. What one thing was created to be was not designed for another thing to do.

I know this all sounds so obvious and simple, but some things are obvious—so obvious that we never really look at them or consider them. Nature is nature. Everything in nature has one primary thing. And every animal or plant or bug or whatever knows it and does it.

We humans are part of nature, and just as everything in nature has one thing that it flourishes in doing, so do we humans. To me, it just seems natural and designed that each of us has one primary thing to be or do. It is simply our natural thing.

That is why we were all born with certain natural talents. Some have great intellectual ability, some have physical talents, and some have intuitive abilities. Some are naturally outgoing; some are naturally quiet and calm. Some have the traits to lead others, some have the traits to work with others, and some have the traits to serve others. And on and on.

We all have things, just like everything else in nature, that we must do and must be to thrive. When we are doing our own one thing, we are simply in our own natural zone. When doing our own one thing, everything flows naturally. Being in the zone is no more than finally doing what you were naturally created to do. It is obvious in sports. It is not as obvious in work or daily life—we may just say that people are good at certain work or certain ways of being.

There is an old saying applicable to my line of reasoning on this theme of natural abilities and nature. When we see someone doing something they are not naturally inclined to do, we say they are "like a fish out of water." It is obvious to us, as observers, that they are trying to do something against their nature.

This highlights why it is so critical for each of us to find our one thing. We humans, compared with other animals, have an amazing ability to adapt to change. Birds do not adapt. If there are no trees to nest in or skies to fly through, they will die off. Tigers do not adapt. If their environment is changed, they can become extinct.

Humans are better at adapting than other animals. Perhaps we should pay attention to the accelerated and unprecedented extinction of wildlife and local animals. In just the past fifty years, more animals have become extinct than ever in the history of the planet. In the past fifty years, over x percent of all animals have disappeared. They could not live the life they were naturally created for, and they became extinct. We humans have survived because we can adapt. But although we can adapt and survive without our one thing, we cannot fully thrive. *Survive* and *thrive* are at opposite ends of the continuum of life. We, as a part of nature, were naturally created for one thing. It is vital for each of us to live and thrive by doing our natural-for-us one thing. Without it, we live, but not at the level for which we were created. I believe that finding our one thing is critical. You and I must be who we were naturally designed to be. We must be our one thing. As a tree must be a tree, you must be you.

# Chapter 3
## Writing Your Story

I hope this workbook becomes the most important workbook you have ever used. Why? Because this workbook has been created specifically to help you to become an author—a writer, author, and most important, creator of your life!

We all know that biographies are usually written from the perspective of looking back on someone's life. This workbook starts not by looking back but with the creation of a life. Your life. This workbook is designed especially for you, to create your story and your new life, starting today.

You have two choices in this world. Write and create your story, or be passive, sit back, become disengaged from your life, and let others write your story for you.

A story is defined as 'a narrative, either true or fictitious, in prose or verse, designed to interest, amuse, or instruct the hearer or reader. We use stories as tactics to get people to see who we are more clearly. Far from simply being a way to differentiate us, our stories help us make decisions, lead, inspire, influence, persuade, build trust, and foster connection.

Psychology Professor Dan McAdams provides us with a simple model for understanding how as humans, our personality develops over time, in three layers. The foundation is who we are at birth and how we develop in early life—our traits. The second layer is our goals and values—what we believe and strive for as we get older. The final layer is our stories—what we choose to remember about our past and how we make it meaningful now and in the future.

He believes we are born actors, begin to develop agency around the age of eight and become authors of our stories in our late teens onwards. McAdams proposes that a person's identity is formed by integrating life experiences into an internalized, evolving story that provides him or her with a sense of purpose. We make sense of who we are by piecing together stories from our reconstructed past, perceived present and imagined future. As Professor McAdams explains, 'In personality psychology, what mainly counts when it comes to the idea of a life story is the narrator's subjective understanding of how he or she came to be the person he or she is becoming.

"To Be or Not to Be"

Even if you have never seen or read a Shakespeare play, you have likely heard this famous quote—"To be or not to be" is the opening line to a soliloquy in the nunnery scene of Shakespeare's *The Tragedy of Hamlet, Prince of Denmark*.

What makes "To be, or not to be" such an enduring quote, still relevant centuries later? Shakespeare was a brilliant person. He was a philosopher and a deep thinker, a wise and learned person. His plays were on the nature of being human and were written in a time, perhaps like today, when society and its ways of thinking were changing and expanding.

Shakespeare honed his skills as a writer. Additionally, he had the gift of being able to write introspectively, the ability to portray the inner workings of the human mind. His writings are successful on two levels: they teach us about ourselves and entertain us as well. His plays engage people and encourage them to think about their lives on a deeper level, rather than the mere surface level.

George Lucas's Star Wars saga in today's time is similar. Star Wars entertains us. But at a deeper level, it teaches us what it is to be human, with all the facets of human character and beliefs.

Looking at Star Wars in the light of deciding on your one thing, which character would you choose to be? Which character would you not want to be? That is the question, isn't it? For in this story of *you*, you get the right to choose your character. In your story, you get to select your part, then go out on life's stage and be that person.

When you were a child, your parents wrote your story. Then perhaps your aunts and uncles and cousins and siblings. Then your friends, teachers, religious figures, and other authority figures in your life. Then you became an adult, and you started to make your own choices and write your own story. But the influences—your environment, your family, and the people in your life—were still in your head, influencing your story. Hopefully, you are now at the point where you are free of those influences, good or bad, and are now writing your own story.

What have you written so far? Have you even started? Are you writing your story, or are you being passive and letting life come along and write it for you? Well, whether you have written something you love or hate or have not even started, let's consider now, this present moment, the start of your new and inspiring biography.

There is only one you. You are different from anyone born so far or who will be born in the future. You are unique, amazing, and one of a kind, and today, with this workbook, you will start uncovering your story and uniqueness. From this moment, you will start writing the story of you.

You have the chance, starting today, to decide if your story will be an inspiring story or a tragedy. A story of failure at each step of your journey or a story of happiness and success each day. You can write your leading part as the hero or the villain.

This workbook is divided into two parts. Part one is about uncovering and deciding on your one thing— the one thing you want to be in your story. In part one of this workbook, you will learn how to choose your one thing, decide on the vision for your life, and think about why that is your purpose. You will think about your vision, mission, and strategy, then decide the best ways to achieve your one thing.

Along the way, each chapter will have questions for you to ponder, answer, and use to create your one thing. Chapter 2 is about how to achieve what you have chosen to do. Life is, particularly in today's tumultuous times, more mental than physical. Part two focuses on getting your mind and thinking focused on success rather than failure. Part two is about how to achieve and create the life you envision. Studies show that top performers—the happiest, most successful people—focus only on what they want in life. Those who are unhappy, frustrated, and not living the story that they want to live focus mainly on what they don't have and don't want. Quantum science teaches us that what we believe something to be is what it becomes. Life is fluid. Reality is created by thought.

This workbook should be your companion for at least the next sixty-six days. Why? Because it takes at least sixty-six days to kill off an old, bad habit and create a new, good habit in its place. And as you will learn, over 50 percent of your success or failure in life is a result of your conscious and unconscious habits. Let's write a story with positive outcomes based on positive, life-affirming habits.

The best way to use this workbook is, first, to spend five to ten days just reading it in full. It is best if you read the workbook over a few days, not all in one sitting. There are scientific studies supporting this method of studying new material.

Then, after the first read, you should read one or two chapters a week, making sure to answer the workbook questions after each chapter.

When you follow this protocol and do the deep thinking needed, you will become the author of your life story. Just as the writing stage of any book is open to edits, be prepared for your storyline to have twists and turns. Let's face it—no one enjoys a boring story. Write an inspiring and action-filled life. Most believe that we each get only one story per lifetime. So write a good one.

WORKBOOK QUESTIONS

1. What character do you want to be in your life?

_____

_____

2. What is stopping you from being that person?

_____

_____

3. Who are role models for you to create your story around?

_____

_____

# Chapter 4
## Myers–Briggs

The Myers–Briggs Personality Type Indicator (MBTI) is an inventory assessment designed to identify a person's personality type, strengths, and preferences.

The MBTI was developed by Katharine Cook Briggs and her daughter, Isabel Briggs Myers. It is based on their work with Carl Jung's theory of personality types. Today, the inventory is one of the most widely used psychological instruments in the world.

Myers and Briggs were fascinated by Jung's theory of psychological types and recognized that the approach could have real-world applications. During World War II, Myers and Briggs began researching and developing an inventory that could be used to help understand individual differences. By assisting people to distinguish personality types, the MBTI helps people select a career or vocation particular to their personality and ways of observing and participating in life.

Myers created the first pen-and-pencil version of the inventory during the 1940s, and the two women began testing the assessment on friends and family.

Based on the MBTI results, people are identified as having one of sixteen personality types. The goal of the respondents is to explore and understand their personalities, such as their likes, dislikes, weaknesses, and strengths, and to discover for themselves their unique career preferences.

A couple of points should be clarified. First, no one personality type is the best or better than any other type. Second, the MBTI is not a tool to look for dysfunction or abnormality. Its purpose is to assist you to learn more about yourself so that you can make rational—not emotional—judgments in deciding on your one thing.

The MTBI is based on four pairs of contrasting traits:

• **Extrovert–Introvert.** This refers to how we function in the world around us. *Extroverts* are "outward-turning" and action-oriented individuals who enjoy more frequent social interaction and feel energized after spending time with other people. *Introverts* are "inward-turning" and thought-oriented individuals who enjoy deep and meaningful social interactions and feel recharged after spending time alone. We all exhibit extroversion and introversion to some degree, but most of us tend to prefer one over the other.

• **Sensing–Intuition.** This refers to how we gather information from our environment. Just like with extroversion and introversion, all people spend some time sensing and intuiting depending on the situation. People with a *sensing* orientation pay attention to reality, particularly to what they can learn from their senses, focusing on facts over intuition. In contrast, those who favor *intuition* focus on patterns and are drawn to and enjoy thinking about future possibilities and abstract ideas.

• **Thinking–Feeling.** This area focuses on how people make decisions. Those with a *thinking* orientation emphasize facts and objective data. They are logical and impersonal when evaluating a decision. Those with a *feeling* orientation base their decisions on emotions.

• **Judging–Perceiving.** The final scale involves how people tend to deal with the outside world. Those who lean toward *judging* prefer facts. People who prefer *perceiving* are more open, flexible, and adaptable.

Taking the MBTI test will provide a window into your personality, which is why the test has become so popular. Even without completing the formal questionnaire, you can probably immediately recognize some of these tendencies in yourself.

Do it well; do one thing at a time

When you are working, work

When you are playing, play

When you are eating, eat

# Chapter 5
## Sixteen Personality Types

No one is more interested in us than us. Personality tests give us a clear insight into ourselves. The 16 Personalities assessment is based on the sixteen personality types developed by Isabel Briggs Myers and Katharine Cook Briggs covered in the last chapter.

The following is my quick overview of the test's sixteen personality types to help you see who you are and, in turn, the one thing that will fit your frame of perceiving, acting, and thinking. We have a link to the 16 Personalities test in a coming Tools section.

**Inspector.** At first glance, Inspector types are intimidating. They appear serious, formal, and proper. They also love traditions and old-school values that uphold patience, hard work, honor, and social and cultural responsibility. They are reserved, calm, quiet, and upright.

**Counselor.** Counselors are visionaries and idealists who have creative imaginations and generate great ideas. They have a different, more profound way of looking at the world. They have depth in their thinking and rarely take anything at surface level or accept things the way they are. Others sometimes perceive them as weird or amusing because of their different outlook on life.

**Mastermind.** Masterminds, as introverts, are quiet, reserved, and comfortable being alone. They are usually self-sufficient and would rather work alone than in a group. Socializing drains an introvert's energy, causing the need to recharge. The Mastermind type likes ideas and theories. When viewing the world, they are always questioning why things happen the way they do. They are excellent at developing plans and strategies because they do not like uncertainty.

**Giver.** Givers are extroverted, idealistic, charismatic, outspoken, highly principled, and ethical, and they connect with others no matter their background or personality. Givers rely on intuition and feelings and tend to live within the realm of imagination rather than in the outside world. Instead of focusing on living in the "now" and what is currently happening, they look toward a better future.

**Craftsman.** The craftsman is most often rational and logical but can also be spontaneous and enthusiastic. Craftsman traits are less recognizable than those of other personality types. Even the people who know them can't accurately anticipate their reactions. At heart, they are spontaneous and at times unpredictable, but they are good at concealing this part of them from others.

**Provider.** Providers are the stereotypical extroverts. They are social butterflies, and their need to interact with others and make people happy usually ends up making them accessible. Providers have a collective personality type and one that is liked by many people.

**Idealist.** Like most introverts, idealists are quiet and reserved. They talk about themselves, especially in the first meeting with someone. They enjoy quiet places. They love analyzing signs and symbols and consider them to be metaphors that have deeper meanings related to life. They can quickly become lost in imagination and daydreams.

**Performer.** The performer is an extroverted, observant, feeling, and perceiving personality. Think of actors, politicians, and public speakers. Performers thrive as the center of attention. They are warm, generous, friendly, sympathetic, and concerned for the well-being of others.

**Champion.** The champion is an intuitive, feeling, and perceiving personality. This personality type is highly individualistic, and champions strive toward creating their own way of moving through the world. Intuitive, they function from their feelings most of the time. They are perceptive and thoughtful.

**Doer.** The doer is an extroverted, sensing, thinking, and perceptive personality. Doers enjoy social interaction and operate by feelings and emotions. They use logical processes and reasoning. Theory and abstract notions don't hold doers' interest for long. Doers leap before they look, fixing their mistakes as they go, rather than sitting idle or preparing contingency plans.

**Supervisor.** Supervisors are organized, honest, dedicated, dignified, and traditional, and they are great believers in doing what they believe is right and socially acceptable. Although the paths toward "good" and "right" are steep, they are glad to take their place as the leaders of the pack. They are the epitome of good citizenry. People look to supervisors for guidance and counsel.

**Commander.** Commanders focus on external aspects. They are like Spock—rational and logical. They rely on intuition but are rational at the same time. Commanders are naturally born leaders. Of the sixteen personality types, they especially need to be in charge. They see the world as full of opportunities and welcome challenges and problems. They have a natural gift for leadership. They thrive on making decisions. They like to come up with off-the-wall options. Ideas flow quickly to them. They are great at starting projects but bad at following through unless they can put a short deadline on the project. They require constant stimulus and challenges. My Myers–Briggs testing reveals the commander type to be my operating type.

**Thinker.** Thinkers are known for their brilliant theories and logic. Thinkers are good at sensing patterns and are therefore good at solving hidden problems that most people miss. They have a natural ability to scan others. They have little interest in mundane day-to-day activities and maintenance. However, when they find an environment where their creative genius and potential gets used, they will work tirelessly to find an inventive solution.

**Nurturer.** Nurturers are philanthropists. They are always ready to help. They are generous and kind to all. They are enthusiastic and unselfish. They value harmony and cooperation and are sensitive to other people's feelings.

**Visionary.** The visionary is one of the rarest personality types. Although extroverts, they don't enjoy small talk. They stick with their group. They are intelligent and knowledgeable. They always require mental stimulation. They like to talk about both theories and facts in extensive detail. They are logical, rational, and objective in their approach to information and arguments.

**Composer.** Composers are introverts who don't act like introverts. They do not connect well with others right away, but when they get to know them, they show their hidden extroverted self. Even if they have difficulties relating to other people at first, they become warm, approachable, and friendly. They can be fun and spontaneous. Composer types live life to the fullest. They live in the present and enjoy new experiences and discoveries. To seek knowledge and wisdom, they will come out of their naturally introverted shell.

*Focus on people—not things*

# Chapter 6
## Learning Styles

Learning styles influence how we learn under different conditions. Some of us learn best by reading about something; others learn best by touching something. One theory of learning styles, again based on the work of psychologist Carl Jung, is presented here for your consideration in determining your life's one thing.

Recall the four main personality traits described earlier:

Extroversion–Introversion

Sensation–Intuition

Thinking–Feeling

Judging–Perceiving

Although each of these dimensions represents a unique aspect of learning style, it is important to remember that your learning style will encompass a combination of these dimensions. For example, your learning style might consist of elements of the extroverted, sensing, feeling, and perceiving learning styles, based on the challenges at that moment.

Extroverted versus Introverted Learning Style

The first component of the Jungian learning styles indicates how learners interact with the outside world. Individuals with an **extroverted learning style** generate their energy and ideas from being among other people. They prefer socializing and working in groups. Learning activities that benefit extroverted learners include coaching and teaching others how to solve a problem. They enjoy collaborative work and problem-based learning. If you enjoy teaching others, participating in a group, and becoming educated through experience, you are probably an extroverted learner.

Individuals with an **introverted learning style** like to solve problems on their own rather than in a group. Introverted learners prefer to take their time before trying something brand new for them. They enjoy solitary, individual work and thinking.

Approximately 60 percent of learners have an extroverted learning style, and approximately 40 percent of learners have an introverted learning style.

Sensing versus Intuitive Learning Style

Those with a **sensing learning style** are more focused on the external physical world versus the inner world of the mind. Individuals with a sensing learning style are realistic and practical. They like order but can quickly adapt to change.

Individuals with an **intuitive learning style** focus on possibilities. Whereas sensing learners focus on the present situation at hand, intuitive learners like to work with options and potential outcomes. These learners like abstract thinking, daydreaming, and imagining the future.

Approximately 65 percent of learners have a sensing learning style, and approximately 35 percent of learners have an intuitive learning style.


Thinking versus Feeling Learning Style

People with a thinking learning style focus more on the structure and function of information and objects. Thinking learners utilize rationality and logic when dealing with problems and decisions. These learners often base decisions on personal ideas of right, wrong, fairness, and justice.

People with a feeling learning style process information on emotions and feelings. People with this learning style enjoy personal relationships, feelings, and social harmony. If you dislike conflict and require harmony, you might have a feeling learning style.

Approximately 55 percent of males and 35 percent of females have a thinking learning style, and approximately 45 percent of males and 65 percent of females have a feeling learning style.

Judging versus Perceiving Learning Style

Individuals with a judging learning style are very decisive. In some cases, these learners make decisions too quickly. They like order and structure and making detailed plans. If you want planning, order, and structure, this may be your learning style.

People with a perceiving learning style adapt and change course quickly based on changing circumstances. They are curious about everything. If you manage to start many projects at once (often without finishing them), avoid strict schedules, and jump into projects first without planning, you might be a perceiving learner. Oh boy, that's me!

Approximately 45 percent of people have a judging learning style, and approximately 55 percent of people have a perceiving learning style.

Please keep in mind that this my summary of learning styles based on my career-coaching experience and seeing firsthand the various personality types in action. To get a perfect understanding of who you are—how you think about, perceive, and navigate this world—you should take the Myers–Briggs test. It is not expensive, and it is one of the best ways to evaluate your strengths and use them to uncover your one thing. Invest in yourself. It will pay dividends for the rest of your life.

# Chapter 7
## A Clear Path

Very few people take a direct and clear path to their one thing. There are some who know what they want to be in life even before starting school. Some want to be a doctor or a firefighter or a nurse. Some know early on that they want to be football players or soccer players or go to the Olympics.

For these few, the path is well defined. There are guardrails and training wheels attached to the path. It's a straight, linear race to the end. They know the rules, the requirements, and the cost in terms of time and effort.

But for the clear majority, perhaps 95 percent of us, we have no clue as to what we want to be or do with our future lives when we start out—there are no guardrails or training wheels; there's no clear path to the end goal.

Most of us rarely even think about it in middle school. Then, just before graduating high school and having to pick a college major, the concept of a career or what we want to do for the foreseeable future jarringly enters our consciousness.

For all of us except the lucky few who know from a young age exactly what they want to be when they grow up, life requires that we discover our natural-born gifts, natural skills, and ways of viewing the world. These attributes are present, but they are hidden from our view. We see the tip of the iceberg, but that vast being of who we are is deep below the surface of our consciousness.

For most people, finding that one thing involves a series of trials and errors. You may pick one thing, thinking it will be the one thing for you, only to find out it's too tedious or boring for your extroverted personality. Or too outgoing for your introverted personality. You may find out that you are a maestro type who likes to do things your way. Or perhaps you are the exact opposite and feel better in a tribe, where you are nurtured and feel safe.

If any of this resonates with you, this workbook is for you. The aim of this book is to help you take a shortcut and bypass years of trial and error. Using today's vernacular, it is a "hack" to discovering who you are and what your personality requires you to do as your one thing. This workbook is designed to help you take a more scientific and educated approach— rather than years of trial and error—to find your career or your one thing. It is my hope for you that this book will clear a path through the woods of unlimited opportunities by revealing your natural talents, skills, and mind-set so that you can start living the perfect one thing that will make you feel excited and fulfilled each day.

*Refine your one thing to one word*

*Tattoo it on your arm*

*Stencil it on a shirt*

*Read it every day*

If the personality tests interest you, there are two that I use in my career coaching. One is free, and the other has a fee.

I would recommend the free one first: 16 Personalities. It is an eye-opening test and gives rich detail that you may delve into further. It can give you a quick and very detailed picture of who you are. Knowing who you are is a giant step toward finding the one thing you want to do in this amazing world of possibilities.

The second one is the respected and much-used Myers–Briggs test. I took it once in my corporate career and once in my entrepreneurial jump; both times, it was an invaluable evaluation tool.

A third option is the just-launched, state-of-the-art One Thing Workbook network, which offers the Online Career Coach. This is a new platform for both mobiles and laptops, so I am slowly rolling it out and inviting people to join. The Online Career Coach, like the 16 Personalities, is free. The difference is that the Online Career Coach is an *interactive* member network that brings together people who are seeking or living their one thing and creates a space for communicating, sharing, and learning together.

## Myers–Briggs

www.myersbriggs.org/home.htm?bhcp=1 16

## 16 Personalities

www.16personalities.com/free-personality-test

## One Thing Workbook

www.onethingworkbook.com

# Part Two: Achieving Your One Thing

vision; mission; strategy

# Chapter 8
## How Do I Start?

How do you start? You start with a plan. If you own your own business, I assume you have created a business plan. If you are an executive at a major corporation, you likely helped create the company's annual business plan. As an executive at a Fortune 100 firm, I created a very detailed financial and operational business plan every twelve months. It took thirty-plus days to complete and required the participation of many people. And if you work for a major corporation, rest assured that your corporation has such a plan—and you are following it—even if they never bothered to share it with you. Businesses just cannot operate successfully without a well-thought-out plan. That plan has three critical pieces: vision, mission, and strategy.

Since leaving the corporate world, I have been what some would call a serial entrepreneur. I have started many for-profit businesses and two nonprofit entities as well.

I will be honest with you. When I sit down and create my business plan on a software application, I always initially struggle to write out my vision. I can quickly create the mission and then the tactics to achieve my mission, but the vision is the nebulous aspect at first.

And right behind thinking about my vision, I have my "why," which is also sometimes difficult to articulate.

Both are hard to capture, at least to me, in words. I know what I want the business to be, but sometimes I really don't have a clear understanding of *why* I want it. And sometimes I cannot clearly write out what the vision for it is. I know what I want to do, but it takes a while to do the "why" and vision thing. But I must, or I cannot communicate it clearly to others. Without that clarity, what I build will be a mishmash. I have learned to stop, before starting to write, and first think hard and long on my "why" and my vision for it. I've done it the other way, and I've learned that starting before I have a clear vision costs me time and money in the end.

I firmly believe that for you to create the life you want, you need to think of your one thing as a holistic plan for work and life combined.

When I first meet with potential coaching or mentoring clients to work with them to uncover and then achieve their one thing, many are somewhat frustrated or confused about the concept of doing one thing. They are somewhat skeptical that it can be done. And they just do not know where to start.

Additionally, they struggle to select just one thing because they have a whole lot of things they like to do or feel they must do.

So instead of asking which of a thousand things they want to do or want to have in their lives, I start by asking two straightforward, strategic questions:

1. Have you created a life plan?

2. Have you thought deeply and written out your vision, mission, and strategy for your life?

Pretty much every time, I get the same two responses. It's either the deer in the headlights look, or they give me the "I could have," "I should have," or "I wish I had" answers.

I then probe and talk with them, not to them, about the need to start the one thing process by creating a strategic, long-view vision for their lives. Then we talk about the next piece of a primary strategy to achieve their long-view vision and why it is critical to have a strategy to achieve a goal. Winning the lottery or waiting for Uncle Bill to kick the bucket and leave his fortune is not a great strategy for success and happiness.

I let that permeate their thinking for a while and move from a cerebral thing to thinking from the heart—

emotions. I ask them how they feel every day, then talk with them about how they want to feel every day. We all think we are damn smart. Some even think they are geniuses. The truth is, however, that emotions and habits determine our lives as much as our minds influence our choices in life. We are emotional beings more than thinking beings.

So, sticking with emotions, we start digging into not what they want to do as their one thing but how they want to *feel* every day, putting aside what they choose to do every day.

WORKBOOK QUESTIONS

1. Have you created a life plan?

_____

_____

2. Have you thought deeply about and then written out your vision, mission, and strategy for your life?

_____

_____

3. What is your vision for your life?

_____

_____

4. What is your mission?

_____

_____

5. What are three strategies to achieve your mission?

_____

_____

6. How do you want to feel every day?

_____

_____

# Chapter 9
## Why Do You Want Your One Thing?

"Very few people or companies can clearly articulate WHY they do WHAT they do. When I say WHY I don't mean to make money—that's a result. By WHY, I mean what is your purpose, cause or belief?"

—Simon Sinek

Have you ever wondered why highly successful people or companies have been able to achieve extraordinary success while others with the same resources have failed? Simon Sinek, in his book *Start with Why*, asks that question. He asks why people like Martin Luther King Jr., Steve Jobs, and the Wright brothers, who had little in common, succeeded in such a grand way. He said they succeeded because they all started with the "why factor."

The question of "why" you want your one thing must be answered if you are to choose a sustainable, empowering one thing. You not only must know what you want, but you also must know why you want it. Although asking the question of why you want your one thing may sound silly to you, it is extremely important for you to know the "why." It is human nature to want to do something now and not want to stop and figure out why we want it. We humans always first choose what we want and then set about getting it. We seldom think first about "why" we want to do it. If people ask you why you want to do what you plan on doing, I will bet you that, at first, you will stumble and have a hard time answering why you want to do your one thing. You can probably talk about what you want for an hour. However, you may have a hard time talking for five minutes about why you must have it.

In selecting your one thing, your "why" must be determined in parallel with your "what." I have learned the hard way that knowing my "why" is just as critical as knowing my "what." The "why" is important is because it will be the driver behind what you want to achieve as your one thing.

Let me give you an example of the need for having both a "what" and a "why." I founded a nonprofit organization. All nonprofits must have a mission statement—a "what." Nonprofits must also have a compelling vision statement—a "why." As a matter of fact, nonprofits will struggle to receive grants and sizeable donations if they cannot tell people not only what they do but also succinctly state why they do it as well. I liken "why" to fuel. A rocket goes nowhere without fuel. Your "why" is your fuel. No fuel, no one thing. When you determine the one thing you want and know why you want it, you can then go after it.

## WORKBOOK QUESTIONS

1. Why did you choose this one thing out of all the things    you    can    do    with    your    life?

_____

_____

_____

2. What motivates you to spring out of bed every morning?

_____

_____

_____

3. Why must you achieve your one thing?

_____

_____

_____

# Chapter 10
## Dig Deep

To pick one thing that will not only withstand the assault of the creative age but also be something that makes you fulfilled, happy, and energized each day, you must think broadly and dig deep. Digging deep is something most people avoid. I have found that the people I coach who develop success faster are the ones who are willing to look inside. They are willing to deal with the discomfort of touching old wounds, knowing that if they can fix them, they can move forward. So as difficult as the questions after each chapter may be, they must be asked and answered for you to select the one best one thing you desire.

Additionally, as you go through this workbook, figure out if your one thing is someone you want to be or, instead, something that you want to do. It can also, at a higher level, be your mission or purpose in life. Look at your one thing as something big you want to do in life, or view it as the person you want to be in life. Think of it as the thing that gets you up in the morning, excited to greet the new day, and as the thing that makes you content at the end of the day. It is the special thing that puts the wind in your sails and the bounce in your walk.

Your one thing is not just another one of the many things you wish you could have, or accomplish, or do. No, your chosen one thing is a big thing, an inspiring thing, a thing that stretches you each day.

Your one thing should be a specific desire that has been arrived at only after much serious thought. Ideally, your one thing will be a lifelong pursuit. Jobs will change, careers will change, especially in these shifting times, but your one thing should be something that will transcend all change. Things move much more quickly in the creative age of today. Industries are being disrupted before our eyes. Like my one thing did, your one thing may change not by choice, but instead by economic disruption.

Additionally, having one thing will bring focus and direction to your busy life. When you know your one thing, you can live with less stress. You will not run around wasting precious time and energy trying to accomplish too many things at once. Nor will you bounce from one thing to the next, quickly abandoning anything that doesn't bring immediate satisfaction. When you have one thing you desire to be or to achieve, you can concentrate each day's efforts on a definite domino to knock down for that day. And each day, each week, each year, you move closer to being or living the life you want to live, being the person you want to be.

In addition to your initial digging deep to determine your one thing, set specific times for regular personal introspection and reflection to assess whether you are on the right track to achieving your one thing. In the beginning, you should evaluate your progress monthly, then quarterly, and finally semiannually. This review process requires that in evaluating your progress toward your stated desire, you must be completely honest with yourself. The main purpose of the evaluation is for you to decide if you need to change your strategies or tactics to achieve your one thing.

Revisions in your one thing should never be made for a minor setback or obstacle. Although your strategies or tactics may need to change at times, a change in your one thing should only be made because of exceptional unplanned circumstances that are beyond your control.

# WORKBOOK QUESTIONS

1. List three things in your life today that are not going the way you want them to go.

_____

_____

_____

2. List three things you can do to change that.

_____

_____

_____

3. What are the five most important things you would like to be doing?

_____

_____

_____

_____

_____

4. How would your life look if you were living your one thing every day?

_____

_____

_____

5. What would you feel like every day if you were living your one thing?

_____

_____

_____

6. What will you give in return for your one thing? (For example, will it be your time, your money, your privacy, or your independence?)

_____

_____

_____

7. Why do you want your one thing?

_____

_____

_____

8. What is your strategic plan for achieving your one thing?

_____

_____

_____

9. What are three strategies you will use to achieve your plan?

_____

_____

_____

10. When you look back on your life, what do you want to be most proud of and pleased for having accomplished?

_____

_____

_____

11. What person or group do you want to help most in this life?

_____

_____

_____

12. What talents, passion, or knowledge do you have to offer the world?

_____

_____

_____

13. If you continue along the same path, where will your life lead you?

_____

_____

_____

14. What weekly and monthly mile markers will you establish to achieve your one thing?

_____

_____

_____

15. What is the largest one thing you can do to earn you the greatest satisfaction in your life?

_____

_____

_____

16. What one thing can you aim for that will benefit the most people?

_____

_____

_____

# Chapter 11
## Hierarchy of Needs

In deciding upon your one thing, you should have lofty goals—the highest aspirations you can imagine. You can't, however, expect to achieve them by magically zipping past the normal rules of time, space, and matter. You should start where you are at this time.

For example, if your one thing is to "help people," and your strategy to do that is to become a medical doctor, that's wonderful. However, if you are just finishing high school, it's obvious that you cannot expect to achieve your one thing of helping people by becoming a doctor immediately. But you should set that as your one thing and start working toward that aspiration.

Additionally, starting where you are at this present time in your life means you must satisfy your hierarchal needs one level at a time. If you are presently at level two now, don't expect to jump to level five before you move up from level three, then level four.

The American psychologist Abraham Maslow proposed, in his theory of human motivation, that healthy human beings have a certain number of needs, and that these needs are arranged in a hierarchy, with some needs, such as physiological and safety needs, being more basic than others, such as social and ego needs.

Maslow's hierarchy of needs is most often presented in a five-level pyramid, as shown in the chapter-opening graphic. In the pyramid, your higher needs will be your target or domino, to be tackled only once your lower, more basic needs are met.

Maslow called the lower four levels of the pyramid "deficiency needs" because they don't affect us when they are met, but we become stressed or anxious if they are not met.

In contrast, at the fifth level of the pyramid, the highest-level need kicks in as it moves a person to "self-actualize" or reach her or his highest, fullest potential as a human being.

Once individuals have met the four levels of deficiency needs, they can turn their attention to self-actualization. Keep in mind that only a small minority of people can self-actualize, perhaps only 5 percent of us. Why? Because self-actualization requires uncommon qualities, such as honesty, independence, self-awareness, total objectivity, outside-the-box thinking, and compassion and love for others without judgment.

Recap: The Five Human Needs

- Physiological needs: hunger, thirst, sex, and sleep.

- Safety needs: job security, protection from harm, and the avoidance of risk. At this level, an individual's thoughts turn to insurance, burglar alarms, and savings deposits.

- Social needs: the affection of family and friendship.

- Self-esteem needs (also called ego needs): divided into internal needs, such as self-respect and a sense of achievement, and external needs, such as status and recognition.

- Self-actualization: famously described by Maslow as follows: "A musician must make music, an artist must paint, and a poet must write if he or she is to be ultimately happy. What a person can be, they must be. This need we may call self-actualization." Self-actualization involves doing things such as going to art galleries, climbing mountains, writing books, and creating art. The theater, cinema, and music industries are all focused on this level. It's the need to help others, care for others, uplift others, teach others, and at the highest peak, awaken others to their highest potential of being.

Self-actualization is different from the other levels of need in at least in one important respect. It is never finished, never fully satisfied. It is, as Shakespeare put it, "as if an increase of appetite grows by what it feeds on."

## First Things First

As I stated earlier, the most important thing to take away from Maslow's hierarchy of human needs, especially in relation to reaching your one thing, is this: you must start fulfilling your needs at the bottom levels of the pyramid first, then, as the needs at each level are fulfilled, you continue up as far as you can rise. The great news is that no matter where you are you today, you have the inner power to raise yourself level by level. No one cannot aspire and reach self-actualization.

## Self-Transcendence

In Maslow's later years, he added an additional higher level of need, a sixth level that he named self-transcendence. The self only finds its actualization in giving itself to some higher goal outside itself, such as in altruism or spirituality. This level represents the desire and need to reach for the ultimate, named by most as God, the universe, or reality. Transcendence refers to the very highest and most inclusive or holistic levels of human consciousness, behaving, and relating, as ends one being. Transcendence involves seeing each human as individual and, at the same time, as one with all others, including all other species and entities: human, animal, nature, and the cosmos.

## WORKBOOK QUESTIONS

1. What are your needs for physical well-being in your life?

_____

_____

_____

2. What are your safety and security needs?

_____

_____

_____

3. What are your social and family needs?

_____

_____

_____

4. What are your self-actualization needs?

_____

_____

_____

# Chapter 12
## Focus

Stop trying to care about *everything*. But do care deeply about finding and focusing on your most important one thing. Focus on the big things, the important things in life. Care only about what is important, not the fleeting or trivial. Don't give a second thought to everything else.

Forget what others think. Forget what others have. Forget about what others do. What do *you* want? Think about what you want, and then focus your precious time and energy only on that one thing.

Never think about what you don't want. Don't focus on what's wrong in your life or what's wrong with the world. Focus on what's good in your life. There is still much good in this world and in your life; focus on that.

You can't have a desire for everything, but you can have a burning desire for one thing. Don't be afraid of life. Don't hide in the darkness of fear. Bathe in the light of possibilities.

This amazing and limitless universe is a blank canvas of endless possibilities for you to do or become. Possibilities are all around you. They are yours to seek, to create, and to realize.

Stop being angry at yourself for always being angry at others and yourself. Don't be angry at others—it does no good. Don't try to fix others—fix yourself. Ironically, when we fix ourselves, we lose the need to fix others.

Accept them for who they are, not who *you* want them to be.

Stop being disappointed in yourself for always being disappointed in yourself. Stop being unhappy for always being unhappy. Get over your ego. Get over your negative-energy feelings. Get over your negative thoughts. They are barriers.

Don't allow things or people to own you. Own yourself. Care for yourself. If you are on solid footing, you can then help others. If you are struggling, how can you help others?

Less is better. More is worse. When I could not stand my corporate career anymore and left it behind, I became free. When I gave a damn, I was owned by my career. I was blind. When I finally owned my own life, I had the confidence and strength to quit. At the height of my career, I chose to become free, and I rose to a new height. I saw the light. It was always there. I just couldn't see it in the darkness.

Fall often. Just get up. Fail often. Just don't quit. The more you fight your fears, the stronger your fears get.

Stop pursuing happiness outside of you. Happiness is inside you, waiting for you to accept and claim it. Stop pursuing enlightenment. You are the light. By pursuing something, you are telling yourself and everyone else that you are not happy and not enlightened. You don't pursue what you already have.

You pursue what you think you don't have. The more you pursue the light, the darker it gets. When you stop chasing what you think you lack, it will chase you.

Don't build more walls of fear in your mind. Knock them down. The mental fears and walls you build are not real. They are an illusion, a very real illusion, but an illusion nonetheless. You create your world. You create what you desire and think about most. The mystics refer to this as Maya. Quantum scientists believe this dimension, this world we sense and see, to be a holistic illusion. It is a projection from your mind to the outside. Illusions are atoms; they are not solid. Let them blow away. The more walls of fear you build, the bigger your prison becomes. The taller the mind's prison of walls, the darker it gets. Your one thing comes when you are outside the walls of your own mind's creation. "Where there are no walls and no damns, the light shines through."

WORKBOOK QUESTIONS

1. Do you worry about what others think? If so, why?

_____

_____

2. What in your life are you fed up with?

_____

_____

3. What stops you from choosing your own life?

_____

_____

# Chapter 13
## Introverts and Extroverts

In choosing your one thing, it's important that you take your personality into consideration in the decision. If, for example, you are an introverted person, you do not want to choose a one thing that involves an extroverted, flamboyant lifestyle. So let's examine your personality. In terms of your energy and interaction with others, there are three personality types: extrovert, introvert, and ambivert.

I have the pleasure of leading a Mastermind group in Atlanta, Georgia. At many of our roundtable meetings, a conversation about one of the members being either an introvert or an extrovert will often arise. The consensus on differentiating the two would usually involve the following points:

- The term *extrovert* relates to how outgoing someone is.

- The term *introvert* relates to how shy or quiet someone is.

This conception was initially close to my general belief as well. But after researching the topic of extrovert versus introvert for one week's Mastermind meeting, my research into Carl Jung, who popularized the terms, found that the common belief is off!

The terms *introvert* and *extrovert* (originally spelled *extravert*) were popularized by Carl Jung in the early twentieth century. However, their meanings got confused between then and now, and we all started thinking that everyone belongs to one camp or the other. But Jung's point was that these are the very extremes of a scale. This means that many people fall somewhere in the middle between introvert and extrovert. People in the middle of the scale are named *ambiverts*.

As Jung noted, "There is no such thing as a pure introvert or extrovert. Such a person would be in the lunatic asylum."

Recent research has shown that the characteristics of introverts and extroverts relate to where we get our energy from—or in other words, how we recharge our brains' batteries.

Introverts (or those with introverted tendencies) tend to recharge by spending time alone. They lose energy from being around people for long periods of time, particularly large crowds.

Extroverts, on the other hand, gain energy from other people. Extroverts find that their energy is sapped when they spend too much time alone. They recharge by being social.

In the 1960s, psychologist Hans Eysenck proposed that the difference between introverts and extroverts was that they simply had different levels of arousal—meaning the extent to which our minds and bodies are alert and responsive to stimulation.

For introverts, external stimulation can be overwhelming. Because their rate of arousal is much higher, they are stimulated easily. Time alone, one-on-one conversations, and predictable situations are more likely to be pleasant for introverts, who are more sensitive to external stimulation.

Introverts are tricky to understand because it's so easy for us to assume that introversion is the same as being shy, when in fact, introverts are simply people who find it tiring to be around other people. For introverts, to be alone with their thoughts is as restorative as sleeping, as nourishing as eating. Introverted people are known for thinking things through before they speak; enjoying small, close groups of friends and one-on-one time; needing time alone to recharge;_and being upset by unexpected changes or last-minute surprises. Introverts are not necessarily shy and may not avoid social situations, but they will need some time alone or just with close friends or family after spending time with a big crowd.

On the opposite side of the coin, people who are extroverted are energized by people. They usually enjoy spending time with others because this is how they recharge from time spent alone focusing or working hard. For example, an extrovert might explain the way she gains energy from being around other people this way: "When I am among people, I make eye contact, smile, and maybe chat if there's an opportunity—like being stuck in a long grocery store line. As an extrovert, that's a small 'ping' of needed energy, a little positive moment in my day."

As mentioned, the ambiverts fall somewhere in between. Introverts and extroverts are the extremes of the scale, and everyone else is in the middle. Many of us lean one way or the other, but there are some who are quite balanced between the two tendencies. These people are ambiverts.

For this research, I took an introvert–extrovert personality test. As it turns out, I fall in the middle—I am an ambivert.

Here is what my test result said: "You're an Ambivert. That means you're neither strongly introverted nor strongly extraverted. Recent research by Adam Grant of the University of Pennsylvania's Wharton School of Management has found that Ambiverts make the best salespeople. Ambiverts tend to be adept at the quality of attunement. They know when to push and when to hold back, when to speak up and when to shut up. So, don't fall for the myth of the extraverted sales star. Just keep being your Ambivert self."

Additionally, ambiverts exhibit both extroverted and introverted tendencies. This means that they generally enjoy being around people, but after a long time, this will start to drain them. I recognize this in myself and even mentioned it, I think, at our last Mastermind. My guess is that some of you are ambiverts as well. Ambiverts enjoy solitude and quiet . . . but not for too long.

Ambiverts recharge their energy levels with a mixture of social interaction and alone time. For me, I can be home alone for two days, working and writing, but on day three, I need to be out and about, meeting with people face to face. If I do not interact with people and have a stimulating conversation, I get tired and agitated and become unproductive because my energy was drained after two days of being an introvert. Being in the middle, I need to spend half of my time as an extrovert and half of my time as in introvert in any given week. I have learned through trial and error that two days inside by myself, working and writing, and then two days outside, meeting with friends and business associates, works very well for optimum, balanced energy and happiness for my psyche.

Although ambiverts might seem to be the more boring personality type, being in the middle of everyone else, this balance can be a good thing. A study by Adam Grant, author of *Give and Take: A Revolutionary Approach to Success*, found that ambiverts perform much better in sales than either pure introverts or pure extroverts. Ambiverts closed 24 percent more sales.

In closing this chapter, I suggest that you may enjoy taking the introvert–extrovert–ambivert test. It's free and available at www.danpink.com/assessment.

Knowing where you are on the scale will allow you to better plan your flow of energy through discharging and recharging your energy throughout the week.

# Chapter 14
## How You Spend Your Days

It has been said that "How we spend our days is how we spend our lives." Every day of our lives is important. No day is to be wasted or taken for granted, for each day makes our lives!

How do you want to spend your days? Above all else, what is the most important one thing for you to spend your days doing? When you look back on your final day, will you say you lived the life you wanted? Of the many things you did, what will be the one thing that really defined you? What was the one thing that made it wonderful for you and for those you loved?

No matter your age, no matter your circumstances, you can still create and live that kind of life now. You are never too young or too old to change. Each day is a new start. No matter what setbacks may have occurred, you can overcome them if you do not stop. Do not stop three feet from the gold.

## WORKBOOK QUESTIONS

1. How do you want to spend your days?

_____

_____

_____

2. What is the most important one thing for you to spend each day doing?

_____

_____

_____

3. How will achieving your one thing allow you to spend each day as you want to live your life?

_____

_____

_____

_____

# Chapter 15
## Good Habits

"People do not decide their future; they decide their habits, and their habits then decide their future."

—F. M. Alexander

You will achieve your one thing by building a new habit. Using the Sixty-Six-Day Journal in this workbook, you will build your one thing success habit day by day for the next sixty-six days.

This chapter discusses how to build a habit. The science-proven fact is that you will only succeed in obtaining, then sustaining, your one thing with the creation of a habit—an automatic, habitual one thing habit.

Although willpower can be used to influence the mind and our actions, habits have just as much influence as well. A Duke University study demonstrated that over 55 percent of what we do is not from "thinking," or willing things to happen, but from habits. This means that over 55 percent of your success in achieving your one thing will be impacted by the habits you currently have.

The bottom line is that for you to achieve your one thing, you are going to have to create a habit of doing it daily for the next sixty-six days. In the journal part of this workbook, you will do some work on your one thing every day for the next sixty-six days. And by doing this for the next sixty-six days, you will be creating a new habit. And by creating a new habit, you will be displacing the old habits that have been holding you back. The fact is that you cannot "break" bad habits through willpower alone. You can only create new, good habits in the place of old, bad habits.

Aristotle said, "We are what we repeatedly do. Excellence, then, is not an act of willpower, but a habit."

I believe that in the acquisition of a new habit, or the leaving of an old one, we must take care to launch ourselves with as strong and decided of an initiative as possible. For you to succeed in developing a new success habit, you must accumulate all the possible circumstances you can for you to create, via a habit, the conditions that encourage your success in achieving your one thing.

And to stay on the path and build a new habit, you cannot rest or break the chain until your new habit is securely rooted in your daily life. Repetition and continuity are key aspects of creating your one thing. If you do not nurture and exercise your new habit daily for sixty-six days, it will wither and die. Journaling and listing the dominos you will topple each day must be done.

Habits take a bit of time to build, but not as much as many people think. Studies have clearly demonstrated that sixty-six days is what it takes to create a habit. We must keep building the habit for at least sixty-six days because it is not the beginning but the moment of the habit producing a modest success that communicates the success to the brain as a "win," and once the brain registers a win, it will start making the habit unconscious and automatic. When the habit becomes unconscious, the effort is lessened, and you are on your way to a new way of acting, thinking, and doing. When your one thing becomes a habit, you will do it each day with little to no effort. You don't have to tell your heart to beat or your lungs to breathe. Both can be thought of as habits the unconscious mind automatically performs for you each day.

Habits, according to neuroscience, emerge because the brain is constantly looking for ways to save energy and effort. Know this: you cannot eliminate a bad habit by sheer force of willpower. You can only create a new, good habit to replace your old, bad habit. The more you understand habits, the less importance you will assign to willpower, goals, and any number of other facets of life that many of the "self-improvement" books center on.

# Part Three: Maintaining Your One Thing

creative shift;  gratitude; live in the present

# Chapter 16
## Two Wolves

Many moons ago, the Cherokee Indian elders were sitting around the campfire on a warm summer evening. The elders were teaching the tribe, especially the young warriors, how to choose the right path in their lives.

One of the wise, elderly leaders talked to the young warriors about the battle that goes on inside each human.

The elder said, "My sons, life's battle is always between the two wolves within us. One wolf thinks only of evil, jealousy, despair, sorrow, regret, greed, inferiority, lies, and hate.

"The other wolf within you thinks only of good, joy, hope, serenity, kindness, compassion, and faith in the future."

One young warrior thought about it for a minute, then asked the wise chief, "Which wolf wins?"

The chief looked at him, smiled, and said, "Only the one that you feed."

In Napoleon Hill's famous book *Think and Grow Rich*, he shows that what we attract to us and thereby create in our lives is *what we think about most.*

The question is, then, Which wolf do you feed each day?

# Chapter 17
## The Shift to Technology

We were not created to be idle or to just get by. We were created for greatness. Like life itself, we were designed to always grow, expand, and move forward. We all need one purposeful, intentional thing to do every day with this gift called life. We all need one thing to work on or work for. We all need one thing in our lives to create, build, play with, or work toward. But how safe is your one thing in a changing world?

The world has gone through three seismic shifts. The first shift was the agricultural age. The second was the industrial age. And the new shift, the third shift, is the creative age. In the last one hundred years of the industrial age, our work was dominated by left-brain ways of thinking. Left-brain thinking is highly analytical, structured, inside the box, hierarchal, controlled, and measured.

In the industrial age, we were expected and taught to be the same—to follow the same playbook and all fit neatly and harmoniously as cogs in the giant wheel of society. The three eras can be simplified as follows:

1. Agriculture age—farmers

2. Industrial age—factory workers

3. Creative age—creators and empathizers

Society has changed dramatically in just the past five years. A seismic shift has occurred. In just the last few years, a tipping point has been reached. An invisible, yet very real line has been crossed. We have entered a new age of work and living—*for the most part, a new age that is still undetected or not understood, even by our academic, business, and government leaders.*

This new era and its array of one things for you and all others to choose from will be dominated by what many are now naming the creative age.

In this creative age, your array and choice of meaningful one things will be dominated not by the old-age guardians at the gates of conformity and structured work, but by creators, idea makers, artists, inventors, designers, storytellers, caregivers, teachers, and big-picture thinkers.

For the past one hundred years, the world of work was straightforward. It was easy to figure out. When you wanted a job, you applied for one, and very soon, you got one. Then you kept it for a long time. Many stayed at the same company for their whole working career.

Well, those days are gone, aren't they? In this new world of work, you can no longer expect to work for only one or two companies. Today, you oversee your own career. Today, you must figure out your one thing and be the creator of it.

The goal of this chapter is to help you see into the future of work and the future of living. This chapter is written to help you chose one thing that is viable not only for the short-term present but for the fast-changing future as well.

We are shifting from economies built on logical, linear, left-brain thinking to economies built on cooperative, conceptual, and creative right-brain thinking. From this chapter, I want you to see that new skills will be needed. To learn more about this new conceptual age, I highly recommend you read the book *A Whole New Mind* by Daniel Pink.

Cheaper, Faster, Better

Work is going to those who can do it cheaper, faster, or better. Today in America, the midrange salary for a chip designer is about $8,000 per month; in India, it's $1,000 per month. In America, a midrange aerospace engineer earns about $6,000 per month; in Russia, an aerospace engineer averages about $650 a month. An accountant in America who earns, say, $5,000 per month would earn about $300 per month in India. In addition to America, this new shift to the creative age in society will impact the entire world. In Germany, Japan, and the United Kingdom alone, it is estimated that this shift will displace over 1.5 million workers.

The realization of cheaper, faster, and better outcomes comes from shifting work out of the country. Or it comes from doing it better with the use of disruptive technologies. Or from artificial intelligence, robotics, battery-powered cars, driverless cars, and algorithms.

Thus, with the new world of work, jobs, careers, and entire industries will disappear. Will your one thing go as well? In that case, you will need to reinvent yourself and create a new one thing. That is why your one thing should be at the highest level, not at the task level. Let me be an example of what I mean by that. As a life coach, my daily tasks are many. I write articles, I write books, I publish books, I do public speaking, and I network. I do job-transition coaching, midlife crisis coaching, business coaching, and entrepreneur coaching. Each one of those is a task. Each of those is a subset of my one thing. My one thing is not any of them, however. They are tasks that make up my one thing. My one thing is "teaching." That is my highest purpose. Teaching how to live an enlightened, intentional life is my one thing.

Therefore, my point is this: when you chose your one thing, select something that is not task oriented, process oriented, or something that is just a section of something bigger. Tasks can be replaced with new technologies. Big things, creative things, cannot. Therefore, as you go through these workbook questions, think big picture. If you think big, the chances are that your one thing will not be disrupted by this rapidly shifting work world. Pieces may change, but a big-picture one thing will always be relevant.

As CEO of FinTech Wealth Group, I research future trends in finance, banking, and technology. Let me give you a clue as to what this creative age will bring in these industries. Robots will one day be smarter than most humans. Today, MBAs are highly valued. Humanities and artists and creators are less valued. In the next ten years, I predict that algorithms, artificial intelligence, and computers will become more intelligent at work than humans.

With the breakthroughs of blockchain technology and cryptocurrency, a new era has arrived. Such advances will take us beyond the technology era and into a new paradigm. New work will come into being as old work disappears. I suggest that you start becoming well versed in blockchain. Your future one thing just may well be a part of this new era.

What will become more valued is things that are outside the current paradigm. This will include creative thinking and internal traits like emotion, empathy, creativity, and heart—the humanistic traits that cannot be replaced by a "Watson" IBM computer. The seat of intelligence will one day soon shift from the head to the heart. Communicating ideas will be a powerful trait for future workers.

WORKBOOK QUESTIONS

In this workbook part, your objective is to determine if your one thing will be part of the new technological and creative age and endure or be part of the passing industrial age and very shortly become obsolete.

1. Do you consider yourself a logical, linear, left-brain thinker or a cooperative, conceptual, and creative right-brain thinker? Explain.

_____

_____

_____

2. Could new or emerging technologies do your job cheaper, better, or faster?

_____

_____

_____

3. How do you think artificial intelligence may eliminate your job or industry?

_____

_____

_____

4. Does your job require creative or inventive thinking, or does it involve simple tasks that can be completed by artificial intelligence?

_____

_____

_____

5. Can a robot or robotics do your one thing better, faster, or cheaper?

_____

_____

_____

6. What disruptive progress may eliminate your industry?

_____

_____

_____

7. Is your one thing in an old-era or new-era industry?

_____

_____

_____

8. How have you prepared to change your one thing when your industry is impacted by the creative shift?

_____

_____

_____

9. Do you have a career backup plan if your job or career is displaced in this new age? If so, what is it?

_____

_____

_____

# Chapter 19
## How to Kill Your Dream

People who fail in life often have one distinguishing trait in common. They know all the reasons for failure and very few of the reasons for success. They have what they believe to be airtight reasons to explain away their own lack of success in business and life.

I call them life's "ifs." Following is a list of the top-seventeen "ifs" I've heard in my thirty-year career of hiring and coaching. As you read the list, determine how many of these "if" excuses you may have used for failing in an endeavor. If you have used them, or if some are currently your go-to "if only" excuses, acknowledge them, get over them, and make it your success goal to never utter "if only" again.

**Top One-Thing-Crushing "Ifs"**

- If only I were younger.

- If only I were older.

- If only I could only do what I want.

- If only I had been born rich.

- If only I had embraced past opportunities.

- If only I could save some money.

- If only my boss appreciated me.

- If only my family understood me.

- If only I had the personality of some people.

- If only I could get out of debt.

- If only I had more money.

- If only I had a better education.

- If only I had good health.

- If only other people understood me.

- If only I could start my life over again.

- If only everybody wasn't against me.

- If only luck was not against me.

# Chapter 20
## Live in the Present

We all think we are fully conscious every moment while we are awake. There is a vast difference, however, between being awake and being conscious. When we are fully conscious, we are present in the moment. We are aware of all that is going around us.

We are observant of all we see and all we feel. We are alert, with clear thinking. We are not fretting about the past or worrying about the future. We are simply fully conscious as an observer in the moment. We are not judging, just observing. If we are in a conversation with someone, we are listening intently to them, not thinking how we are going to rebut or respond to their words.

You cannot tell it just by looking at people, but nearly everyone you encounter is not fully present as they interact with you. Even as people talk to you, there may be a program or script running in the back of their minds, thinking anxiously about the future or regretting past thoughts or actions.

It's hard not to feel anxious about the future because today everything is so frustratingly uncertain and constantly changing.

So how do you stay focused on achieving your one thing and stay present in each moment? One way is to be conscious and recognize when those distractions, frets, and worries pop into your mind; let them pass, and bring your thoughts back to right now. Think, *What I can do right now to best achieve my one thing?*

Just remember that worrying, stressing, fearing, and fretting will only take away precious energy from the current moment. It will never solve the problems of the past or the worries you have for the future.

# Chapter 21
## Hang Out with Uplifting People

We are influenced not only by our habits and continual thoughts. We are also influenced by our family, friends, work associates, and the total environment that we live in.

When I am around negative-thinking, low-energy, argumentative people, I become drained of my energy force, and I feel sapped rather than feeling empowered or optimistic. Sometimes when my mentoring or coaching clients live only in negative energy, I have to fire them. You cannot open closed minds. You can be an example, you can teach, you can love them, but sometimes you cannot save them from themselves.

However, when I am around people who are good for me or in an environment that I resonate with on a high level, I suddenly have more opportunities flow to me.

As mentioned, I lead Mastermind groups. In each group, we focus on helping each other stay conscious and see the good in life. Over and over, when we are all in sync, we bring opportunities to each other. Over and over, by uplifting people, we create an energy force that exponentially multiplies. It seems those who think positive and act in a positive way create positive things in their lives. And those who feel powerless and act powerless bring negative results to themselves.

After many corporate years of being around people who were not good for me, I now enjoy the compounding that happens when I am around people I enjoy, respect, and love.

You can't change all the people around you, but you can subtly influence them in a meaningful and positive way. Perhaps a genuine smile to everyone you encounter may raise someone's spirits that day. That is a step in the right direction. If you just bring positive, loving energy to three people a day, over a lifetime, you will have changed the world.

# Chapter 22
## Start with Gratitude

The concept of gratitude being part of a successful and happy life has now entered mainstream thinking. Not long ago, it was considered a little woo-hoo or not a part of hard-core success-oriented thinking. That has changed, and many people are incorporating gratitude as part of their daily agenda, just like healthy eating, yoga, and meditation practice.

Considering Maslow's pyramid, you can express gratitude in all levels of your needs and desires for growth. For example, you can start thinking daily of three things you are grateful for in the first level of your basic physiological needs. You could be grateful that you have a home to live in, for instance—some do not. Or that you have healthy food to eat three times a day—some do not. Or that you have robust health—many do not.

I suggest here that you go back to the chapter on the hierarchy of needs. Look at the levels, and think about three things you are grateful for at each level you have achieved. As you engage with this workbook, this should be part of your ritual each day.

Expressing gratitude seems a natural human response. So why is gratitude not a part of everyone's—and perhaps your—daily life? Is it possible that your active, fast-paced days and many distractions make forgetting to be aware of all the good in your life seem like nothing special?

What Is Gratitude?

Gratitude is recognizing the favorable things or positive life experiences you have today in your life.

Is Gratitude an Attitude?

Gratitude is a major part of my daily life. I start from the time I wake up, even before I am out of bed. I simply say, "Thank you, God, for another day." When I have my morning coffee in my office, I settle into my well-broken-in leather chair and just let my mind flow and think of the things I see and note how grateful I am to see them in this moment. Simple things like the flowers and trees outside my window. Our dogs at my feet, waiting for a treat. The gift of being healthy and the opportunity to be able to write for a couple of hours before I start my day. Grateful thinking is simple to do. After a while, it comes naturally. It is a way to approach the day in a good mood. Previously, I would start the day thinking about what I had to do and whether I could get it all done. I started out on a worried, negative note, not like now with a gratefulness mind-set. It has changed the flow of my entire day.

True, not contrived, gratefulness thinking is a natural feeling that surfaces from within. Many people describe being grateful—or ungrateful—each day as a choice. And as a choice, gratitude is an attitude and is more than an emotional response.

Being grateful for the things in our lives and world takes a certain amount of gracefulness, a certain amount of humility. Look all the aspect of your life— everything that is worthwhile that you are receiving. For example, consider how many people and things were involved in producing the clothes that you are wearing right now—from the person who planted the cottonseed to the millions of organisms that were involved in making the plant grow; from the people who prepared the cotton, from ginning to weaving to spinning, to the clothing maker, agent, distributor, and seller.

Consider the daily food you eat. Are you grateful for it and the people who participated in bringing this to you?

If you are aware of this and if you receive gracefully, you will be overwhelmed with gratitude. Gratitude is not just an attitude; it is something that, if you are aware of everything in your life, just flows out of you. Gratitude is not forced; it simply happens when you are aware of and overwhelmed by the people and things that are in your life.

Everything in life is, without your effort, collaborating to keep you alive and well right now—from your breath to the food that you eat, to the sun rising and setting. If you were able to see the vastness of it all, you could not help but be filled with gratitude for all the people and events happening to support you as you go through each day.

Gratitude practiced naturally throughout each day will be a very real connection that helps you to achieve your one thing. I ask you to be mentally open to practicing gratitude every day. Do it for sixty-six days, and watch how your thinking changes for the better.

These ten simple "baby steps" will help you start feeling more grateful and appreciative of the good things in your life:

1. Notice good things in your life. Look for them; appreciate them.

2. Savor, absorb, and really appreciate those good things.

3. Express gratitude to yourself or someone else for bringing the good things you notice into your life. Be grateful each day for the work you did to achieve your one thing today or for something related to your one thing that came to you even without your effort.

4. Notice the small, everyday details of your life, recognizing the good things you might many times take for granted.

5. Each day, think of three things you are grateful for. Nature. People. Community. Shelter. Creature comforts like a warm bed or a good meal. It's amazing what you notice when you focus on feeling grateful.

6. Start a gratitude journal. Make a commitment now to writing down good things each day.

7. Let gratitude open your mind to notice good things as they happen.

8. Show genuine appreciation to someone who did something nice for you during the day. Look for opportunities to "pay it forward." Hold the door open for the person behind you, show patience to a struggling cashier, or occasionally pay for someone's morning coffee in the drive-through line behind you at Starbucks.

9. Tell people in your life how you feel about them and what they mean to you.

10. Every day, practice gratitude. As you move through your day, pause now and then when you remember, and think as you do something, "I am grateful."

# Chapter 23
## Never Stop

Never stop working on your one thing. In the still-top-selling self-help book written many years ago titled *Think and Grow Rich* (eighty million copies sold), the author, Napoleon Hill, tells of a man named R. Darby who had one thing that he wanted. He wanted to be rich. So, Darby ventured out West with his uncle to try his luck during the Colorado gold rush. At first, he struck it rich, but the vein of gold petered out, so he lost interest, gave up, and sold his gold-mining equipment for pennies on the dollar to a junk dealer, then hopped a train back home.

The junk dealer hired an expert geologist. The junk dealer drilled where the expert suggested and struck the mother lode of gold . . . *just three feet from where Darby and his uncle stopped digging.*

R. Darby was later interviewed and shared his story of quitting too soon. He attributed his later vast success in the insurance business to the life lesson he learned from abandoning his dream too soon. He said that he could now accept that sometimes things would become difficult, and sometimes he would lose, but never again would he ever give up on his life's goal.

# Closing Thoughts

## The Five Mysteries

When you become self-aware of the five mysteries, you will have found your one thing.

You will have found the following:

1. Who you are

2. What you are a part of

3. Your life's purpose

4. What difference you must make while here

5. What goodness you will leave behind

# About Author

Steven is a prior fortune 100 executive, death survivor, author, mentor and founder of Green Pets America Charities, whose vision is to end the euthanization of shelter animals in America.

Steven's additional books include Project Black Dog Adoption, Bitcoin Guide for Virgins, Art of the Black Dog, Rescue Renew Rehome, and Chasing Love.

# Mentoring references for

# Steven Monahan

Tom Cramer, CEO Coaching; Founder, The Brain Trust; Co-Founder, Wisie, Inc.; Co-Founder, Interactive Assets, Inc. Steve is an idea man extraordinaire. Trust this socially conscious man to guide you and nourish your purpose. He is a very successful businessman who is now taking those outstanding skills and applying them to helping people live better lives.

Sherry Richardson, CEO, Richardson Automotive. Hiring Steven Monahan as my consultant and coach has been very beneficial for me. I made a major business, life, and financial changes in my life. I sold my thirty-year-old business and had to overcome the deep anxiety of what to do next in my career and life. Steve compassionately and quickly helped me get my answers. Mike Sena, CFP®, Author, Wealth Manager, Avid Polo Player. Steve has been a mentor to me for a number of years now. Steven has been instrumental in helping me focus on my business plan, executing it more effectively, and attracting good-fit clients.

Corinna Murray, DVM, CPC, EL-MP, Veterinary Care Navigation and EnHABiT. I met Steve on LinkedIn when I was compelled to connect with him after I read some of his intelligent and provocative articles. He is compassionate, gracious, and fierce about what he believes, as are his articles. Steve tirelessly creates ideas and has a generous spirit that is as contagious as his generous smile.

Jon Cooper, CEO, DIGB. Steve is a warm and compassionate human being. He leads with vision and wisdom. Steve is always there to lend a helping hand. Process oriented, attention to detail, and results driven are only a few of the many attributes Steve has in his arsenal; he never lets his focus stray from the task at hand.

Jeff Snow, Business Owner, Director, Cherokee Toastmasters. Steve joined Cherokee Toastmasters, and he became an outstanding speaker and leader in his vision for his community. Steve has coached me personally with my business. Steve uses his extensive business skills and talents to help me excel.

Marilyn Cramer, Founder, Light Healer, LLC. Steve is a compassionate, results-driven, caring person. Steve has a great work ethic and great astuteness when it comes to business. Whatever he touches turns to gold. It is a great honor to know Steve . . . he is wise, kindhearted, and considerate.

---

*Steven has been recognized by community, business, and governmental entities along with the State Senate of Georgia and the City Council of Woodstock for his service to his community.*

Lightning Source UK Ltd.
Milton Keynes UK
UKHW021538140120
356931UK00010B/2108/P